GUITAR TUNING

FOR THE COMPLETE MUSICAL IDIOT

ISBN No. 0-89898-118-2

Special thanks to the GIBSON PEOPLE for letting me use part of their book
"Gibson Authoritive Guide to Guitar Strings"

2 HANKIES

CONTENTS

Everything You Need To Know 4

Thumb Rules 5

Pitch 6

Pitch Pipes 7

Harmonic Tuning 8

Tuning Forks 9

Tuning To A Piano 9

The Most Common Way To Tune 10

Tuning By Chords 11

Tuning To The Record 11

Tuning By Beats 11

Octave Tuning 12

Tuning The 12 String 13

Pure Tuning Versus Equal Temperment 14

The Last One 15

Changing Strings 16

Picky, Picky, Picky, All About Picks 17

Defining Intonation 18

Electronic Tuning Devices 21

Using The Tuning Devices To Correct Intonation 23

String Smarts 24

Finding The Right String For You 27

Windings, Round And Flat 28

String Materials And Tone Color 29

Common String Questions 30

Everything You Need To Know & A Lot Of Things You Don't.

Is there anything worse than hearing a band or someone play out of tune? Sometimes it seems like it takes ages to tune up and sometimes we still can't get it just right, so we blame it on our "tin ear" or we say "I'm tone deaf" or how about "I'm just not musical". This book is about the art of tuning. We'll cover every aspect of it. The various ways and methods available to tune your instrument whether it's the guitar, bass, and even the 12 string guitar. Try all the methods and you'll soon be choosing one or two that's your favorite. There's also a section on electronic tuning devices. And for those that really can't hear to tune up, we've enclosed a record so that you can actually "hear" the pitch of the strings and tune to the record.

We'll discuss proper intonation in detail and how to be in tune all over the guitar neck.

There's a section on strings, selecting the proper strings is crucial to your playing. The wrong type can make playing difficult, project sound poorly, and go out of tune too often.

We'll even talk about picks, guitar picks, and what they do to strings.

Once you learn to tune, and it is a learned experience to tune up properly and quickly, it will make a positive difference and give you more confidence in your playing, so let's take it from the beginning …

FOOLPROOF GUITAR TUNING METHOD

By Stephen Funk Pearson

To Tune **A** String   Use A440 tuning fork

(While both strings of the below pairs are sounding, tune the appropriate string until the undulating beats disappear.)

To Tune **Low E** String   Harmonic at 5th fret on Low E string
                                  Harmonic at 7th fret on A string

To Tune **D** String   Harmonic at 5th fret on A string
                                  Harmonic at 7th fret on D string

To Tune **G** String   Harmonic at 5th fret on D string
                                  Harmonic at 7th fret on G string

To Tune **B** String   Harmonic at 7th fret on Low E string
                                  Open B string

To Tune **High E** String   Harmonic at 7th fret on A string
                                  Open High E string

CREDITS

Opening musical fragment: *"Brunella The Dancing Bear"* composed by Stephen Funk Pearson, published by Theodore Presser Co., recorded on *"Hudson River Debut"* record album, KYRA Records, Highland, N.Y. 12528-1215

Instruments: John Gilbert classical guitar, Martin D-35 steel string acoustic, Fender Stratocaster electric guitar

Strings: D'Addario J46, J17 and XL110

Recording engineer: Aaron Hurwitz

TUNING THE GUITAR

How to tune your guitar even if you're tone deaf.

Let us begin by saying that although you may be "tone deaf" now, it's not always a permanent condition . . . A sense of pitch, of being able to detect when a note is too high or too low, can be developed through practice. Although some people are born with "perfect pitch," somewhat like being born with a photographic memory . . . most of us are not that lucky. The best we can hope for is to develope "relative pitch." With relative pitch, a guitarist can tell by playing one note, what the other notes should sound like. This ability is not so much a gift of the gods as it is a skill acquired after a good deal of practice.

THUMB RULES

1. Pick the string and wait a few seconds before tuning. A guitar string is sharp when it is first picked, and then tends to settle down.

2. Tuning the guitar takes **daily tuning practice**. You have to train the ear. Keep practicing.

3. Tune slowly and listen very carefully to the sound or beat of each note.

4. When you tune a string and you just can't seem to hear the right pitch, you might have gone past it. Stop, and turn the turning key back 3 or 4 full turns and start over.

5. If only to accompany yourself on the guitar, the main thing is to get the guitar **in tune to itself** (relative pitch). It does not have to be in absolute pitch.

PITCH

The pitch of a sound depends only on the frequency of the vibration by which it is produced. It does not depend on the nature of the vibration. Thus we may say that it is the frequency of vibration that determines the pitch of a sound. If there is no clearly defined frequency, there is no clearly defined pitch, because the sound is no longer musical.

If we experiment with a series of forks tuned to all the notes in the middle octave of the piano, we shall find the following frequencies:

c	261.6	f	349.2	a	440.0
c#	277.2	f#	370.0	a#	466.2
d	293.6	g	392.0	b	493.9
d#	311.1	g#	415.3	c'	523.2
e	329.6				

Such, at least, are the numbers of vibrations for tuning forks or any other instruments tuned in **"equal temperament"** to the new (1939) internationally agreed pitch of a = 440. But many other standards of pitch are still in use, and even more were in use in the past. The lengths of old organ-pipes give us information as to the pitches which were in use in early times, and shew that one and the same note often had very different frequencies in different instruments. In Germany, for instance, Silbermann's great organ in Strassburg Cathedral (1713) had the pitch a = 393; while Schnitger's organ in S. Jacobi in Hamburg (1688) was tuned to a = 489 — nearly four semitones higher. And this was not the worst, for the "church pitch" of Northern Germany had been given by Pretorius (1619) as a = 567, which is a full six semitones higher than that of the Strassburg organ. Not only so, but secular music was often played in a substantially higher pitch than sacred music, so that there was a "chamber" pitch which was quite distinct from the "church" pitch. There were similar variations in other countries. In England, Father Smith's organ in Trinity College, Cambridge, was tuned (1759) to a = 395, while Berhardt Schmidt's organs in Durham Cathedral and the Chapel Royal gave a = 474.1 — more than three semitones above the Trinity organ.

Early in the eighteenth century efforts were made to make musical pitch more uniform, but it still ranged from about 415 to 430 for a. It stayed fairly stationary within these limits for about a century, when musicians, striving for greater brilliance and keenness of tone, began again to raise the frequency.

RELATIVE PITCH is when the guitarist may guess at the pitch of the string he tunes first and tunes the other 5 strings in relation to that one. It is then in tune with itself. A 17th century lutenist named Thomas Robinson advised setting the pitch of the high string with the instructions "Tune the Treble (first string) as high as you dare without snapping."

ABSOLUTE PITCH is the exact pitch of a note in terms of vibrations per second to produce a given tone.* To tune to absolute pitch you must use a tuning fork, pitch pipe, or an electronic tuning device to have a starting pitch that one of the strings can be tuned to. The other 5 strings are tuned in relation to the string tuned to absolute pitch.

*A-440 vibrations per second.
*E-329.6 vibrations per second.

PITCH PIPES

There's an old saying: "The one great advantage of a pitch pipe over a piano is it's easier to fit in your guitar case."

The guitar pitch pipe has the advantage of being small, light in weight, inexpensive and gives the guitarist the approximate pitch of each string.

The pitch pipe is a device made up of cylindrical reed pipes joined together and lettered to identify the pitch when air is blown through each individual reed.

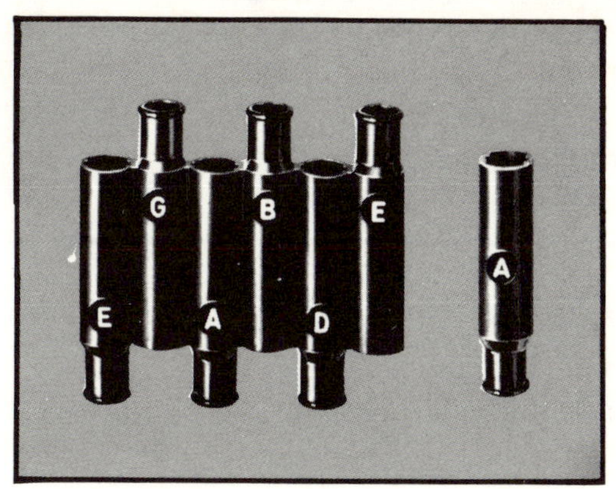

There are single note pitch pipes (A or E) and 6 note pitch pipes for each string on the guitar.

The guitar pitch pipes often go out of tune. Occasionally some of the individual pipes may become clogged and useless. If you use a pitch pipe, try tuning only one of the strings to get the pitch then tune the other strings to the one string that has been tuned.

FINGER PRESSURE WHEN TUNING

Sometimes we press too hard, stretching the string excessively and producing a sharping effect. Be careful to put your finger straight down on the string and to not pull the string to either side. (Try to keep a light touch in your playing too.)

Fig. 1 shows the proper pressure.

Fig. 2 shows the added stretching that occurs when excessive pressure is used.

Fig. 1

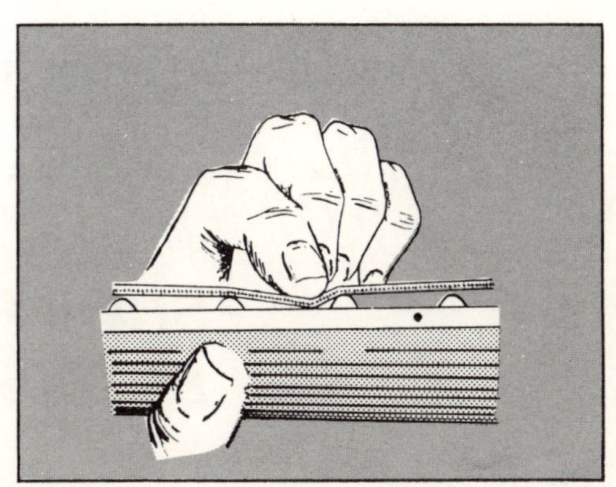

Fig. 2

HARMONIC TUNING

One of the most natural "Special Effects" on the guitar is the "Harmonic" note. It is that chime or bell-like sound you often hear a guitarist play. The harmonics are sustained tones produced by lightly touching your freting hand finger to specifis places on the strings. Try it on the 12th fret, that's the easiest place. Just a light touch, **(not pressing)** directly on top of the fret, after the string is picked, quickly take your finger off. If done correctly that nice bell-like tone will sound and you have just divided the string into 2 sections. This is called the first overtone (see pages 24 and 25 for more on overtones). Try it on all the strings at the 12th fret just for practice. ——→

Other positions will produce the natural harmonics and can be used to tune the guitar. Here you will sound the matching pairs on two different strings and tune by eliminating all "tremelo" or "beats" from the combined sound.

1. Start with a "A"tuning fork to tune the 5th string. If this is not available use Relative Pitch (see page 6) and continue with the steps below.

2. Match the sound of the harmonics of the 5th string, 7th fret with that of the 6th string, 5th fret.

3. Match the sound of the harmonics of the 5th string, 5th fret with that of the 4th string, 7th fret.

4. Match the sound of the harmonics of the 4th string, 5th fret with that of the 3rd string, 7th fret.

5. Match the sound of the harmonics of the 3rd string, 4th fret with that of the 2nd string, 5th fret. This sound may be difficult for inexperienced players to make so an alternative is produced by matching the 6th string at the 7th fret to the open 2nd string.

6. Match the sound of the harmonics of the 2nd string, 5th fret with that of the 1st string, 7th fret.

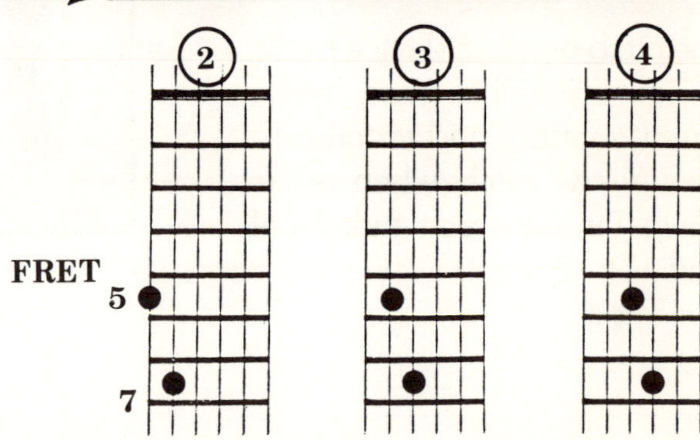

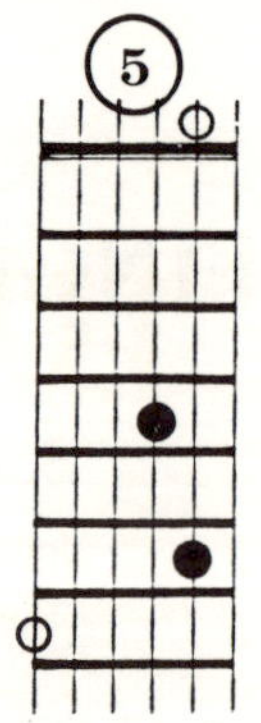

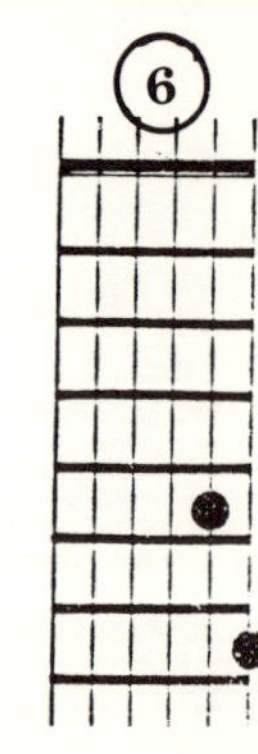

STRANGE FACT: #1

Before the development of printing, Italian barbershops had guitar-like instruments for customers to play while waiting.

SHORTLY AFTERWARDS, COMIC BOOKS WERE INVENTED.

TUNING FORKS

The tuning fork is held between the thumb and index finger. One of the prongs is struck against a solid but resilient object. The rubber heel of a shoe or the players knee. This forces the prongs to vibrate

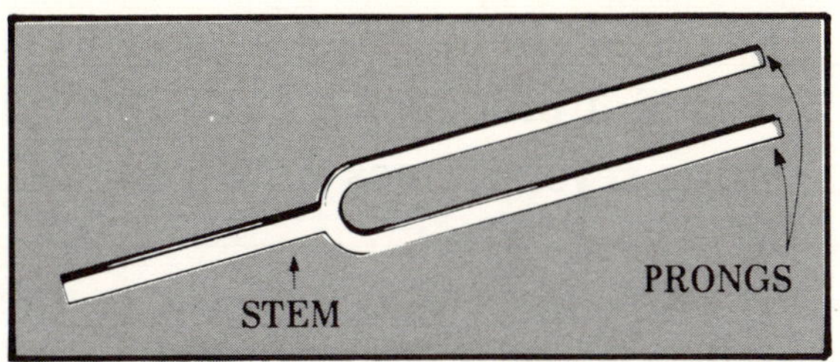

rapidly. Then place the stem against the bridge or other surface of a hollow body guitar. The guitar will then vibrate in sequence with the fork, or hold the fork close to your ear to hear the musical pitch. There are several pitches of tuning forks available. The most common and recommended is the A-440 and E-329.6. The prongs when struck will vibrate back and forth 440 times each second. The tuning fork has great permanency of pitch and is one of the most used tuning devices for musicians. The fork should not be struck against a music stand or the edge of a table or any other hard object. Also do not nick or scratch the tuning fork as it will get out of tune.

TUNING TO A TUNING FORK

The 1st string at the fifth fret is "A" on the guitar. It vibrates at the rate of 440 vibrations per second. The other "A" is the harmonic "A" on the 5 string fifth fret. Hit the fork and tune the string to it and then follow one of the other tuning methods for the other strings or use the E fork for the first string and then follow the most common way to tune.

TUNING TO A PIANO

The piano will give the guitarist the relative pitch of each string. Most likely the piano will not be in tune with itself and therefore out of tune with absolute pitch, so when using the piano for tuning just tune one string to it (the first) and then tune the other strings to that string.

Follow the diagram if you want to tune all of the strings to the piano.

Locate "E" (two white notes up from middle "C"). Strike that key, listen to the pitch. Now, pick the open first string and tune it until it matches the pitch of the piano. Working down the piano keyboard, tune the other five strings in the same fashion.

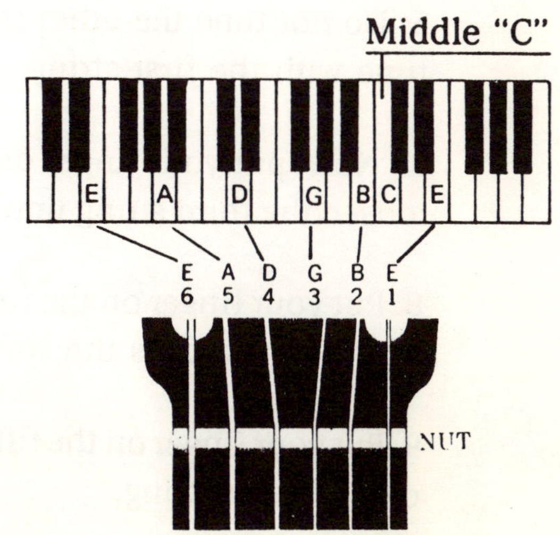

THE MOST COMMON WAY TO TUNE
TUNING TO RELATIVE PITCH OR
USE THE E OR A TUNING FORKS FOR ABSOLUTE PITCH

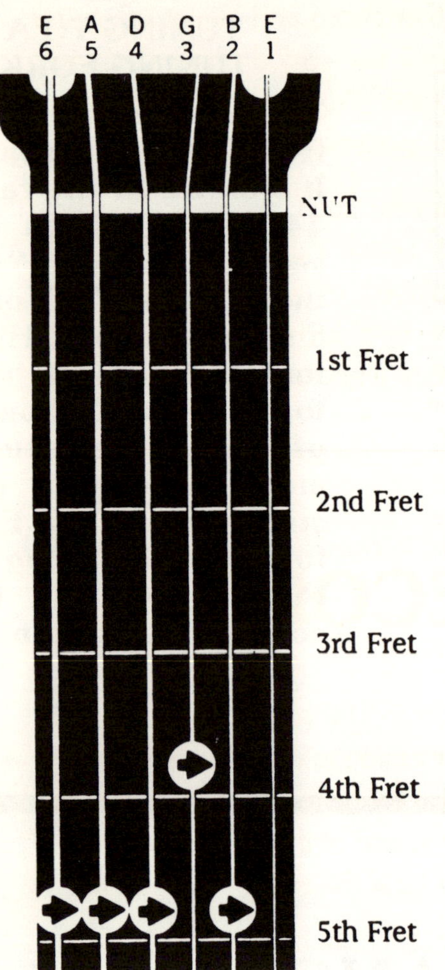

1. Loosen or tighten the first string (the thinnest one), striking it until it produces a fairly high-pitched tone. Strike the first string several times until you can remember the pitch.

2. Press down on the second string — at the 5th fret down from the top — and strike the second string. Listen carefully to the pitch. Is the pitch of the second string higher or lower than the unfingered first string? It is helpful to hum the pitch of one string and then the other. When you hum the pitch of the second string, listen to your own voice . . . does it rise or drop in comparison to the humming of the first string?

3. If you think that the fingered second string is <u>lower</u> in pitch, slowly tighten the second string, listening carefully until it matches the open first string.

4. If you think the fingered second string is <u>higher</u> than the open first string, loosen the second string until it is lower in pitch than the open first string. Now, slowly tighten the second string until it matches the open first string.

5. The "tuning habit" is an important one to develop. You will use the same method for tuning the other strings. Remember: You tune the string on which your finger is placed.

6. Do not tune the other strings until you feel sure the second string is in tune with the first string.

7. Now, put your finger on the third string, 4th fret, and slowly tighten or loosen the third string until it matches the sound of the open second string.

8. Put your finger on the fourth string, 5th fret, and slowly tighten or loosen it until it matches the sound of the open third string.

9. Put your finger on the fifth string, 5th fret, and match it to the sound of the open fourth string.

10. Put your finger on the sixth string, 5th fret, in the same manner as the other strings, tune it to the sound of the open fifth string. Your guitar is now in tune.

TUNING BY CHORDS

Play a chord and tune the guitar for that chord. Then switch to another chord and adjust the guitar again. Use different positions of the same chord and also chords that use varied finger positions. Make sure the chords of the key in which you are playing sound good. Tune using mostly minor chords, since they are closer to being pure in the system of equal temperament than major chords.

Tuning by chords compensates for imperfections and irregularities such as the acoustical compromises of the system of equal temperament, strings that aren't exactly perfect, slight mislocation of the nut or saddle, frets that are worn or slightly misplaced, or deviations caused by adjustment of the action. In addition to its technical advantages, tuning by chords is more beautiful to the ear than other systems. Segovia tunes by chords and tell guitarists who tune by unisons or by harmonics that it is unaesthetic to sit and pick notes out of the air.

TUNING TO THE RECORD

The strings are numbered 1 through 6 beginning with the thinnest string. The sound sheet will have the notes for tuning your guitar. Just match the pitch of the string your tuning to the one on the sound sheet. You'll hear each string played three times. Turn the tuning key for each string until the sound of the string matches the sound of the recorded one. You'll also hear the sound of the "E" tuning fork for **absolute pitch** and then you can use "the most common way" to tune the rest of the strings.

So you can practice tuning to the piano, we've included the notes on the piano too.

TUNING BY BEATS

Tuning by beats requires ears that are very sensitive. When striking the two notes together, if the two notes are not in tune with each other the volume or intensity of both the notes will increase and decrease in regular succession. The periods of maximum intensity are called beats and separated by fairly distinct pauses. Listen carefully and you will hear them.

The number of beats per second is equal to the difference in vibrations per second of the notes. The slower the beats, the closer the pitch of the two notes. When you can't hear the beats the two tones are identical and in tune.

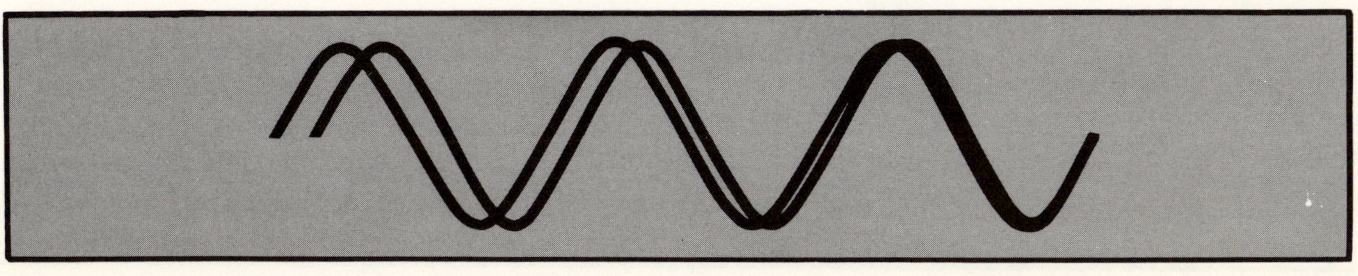

OCTAVE TUNING

An octave is the interval between the first and eighth notes of the diatonic scale. Notes that are an octave apart are called by the same letter name. The upper note will have exactly twice the number of vibrations of the lower one. So that being true, this tuning is not really octave tuning but everyone calls it by that name so. . .we follow.

This is tuning with one open string and the other one fretted. Remember the human ear detects flatness more easily than sharpness, if two strings are not quite in unison most people will raise the pitch of the lower one, thinking it to be flat. Just take your time and go slow.

1. Fret and pick the 1st string at the 7th fret. While it's ringing out pick the 2nd string open. Now with both strings ringing out reach over with your picking hand and tune the 2nd string to match the first string. When you have those tuned move to step number 2.

2. Fret and pick the 2nd string at the 8th fret and the 3rd string open, tune these two together.

3. Fret and pick the 3rd string at the 7th fret and the 4th string open, tune these two together.

4. Fret and pick the 4th string at the 7th fret and the 5th string open tune these two together.

5. Fret and pick the 5th string at the 7th fret and the 6th string open, tune these two together.

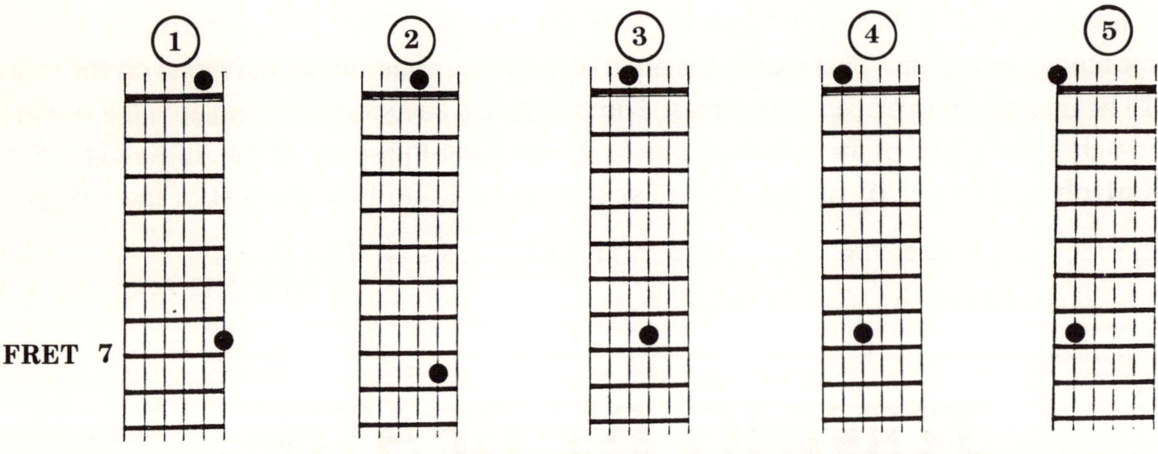

TUNING THE 12 STRING

The 12 strings on the guitar can be tuned to the standard pitch of the 6 string guitar, just use light gauge strings. However some guitarists prefer to tune their 12 strings, two (2) or three (3) semi-tones **lower** than the standard pitch because of the great tension and stress of the 12 strings on the neck, the sounding board and the bridge. Tune as accurately as possible so that the unison and octave notes will be heard clearly.

1. Use the "most common way" to tune this is the pattern you will tune the 12 string with.

2. Start on the first string of the first pair (the thinest). Bring it up to pitch using the sound sheet, pitch pipe, tuning fork, etc. When it's in tune, pick both strings together open, slowly tuning the second string of the first pair until it sounds like the first string.

3. Tune the second string using the most common way.

4. In tuning the 3, 4, 5 and 6 pairs of string, tune the thicker or heavier string **first** and then tune the smaller or thinner string to it. Remember the smaller string is an octave apart.

STRINGS as there, can be variations in tuning. There can be variations in the strings used. You may want to experiment in the type, i.e., bronze, silk and steel, flatwonnds, brass, nickel. And gauges, i.e., extra light, light, medium. To get the tone and ease of playing you like the most.

RECOMMENDED TUNINGS

Strings and Relative Tuning	Standard Guitar Pitch	2 Semi-Tones Below Guitar Pitch (See Note A)	3 Semi-Tones Below Guitar Pitch
1st pair - in unison	E	D	C#
	E	D	C#
2nd pair - in unison	B	A	G#
	B	A	G#
3rd pair - octave apart (See Note B)	G	F	E
	G	F	E
4th pair - octave apart	D	C	B
	D	C	B
5th pair - octave apart	A	G	F#
	A	G	F#
6th pair - octave apart (See Note C)	E	D	C#
	E	D	C#

NOTES:

A. With this tuning, when you finger an E chord it will sound as a D chord; when you finger an A chord, it will sound as a G chord, and so on.

B. For 3rd pair of strings, some players prefer to tune to unison, using 2 identical 3rd plain (not wound) strings.

C. In the 6th pair of strings, some players tune the strings two octaves apart. This requires the use of a guitar E or 1st string, in place of the D or 4th string mentioned above.

12 STRING GAUGE GUIDE

EXTRA LIGHT	LIGHT
.008	.009
.008	.009
.010	.012
.010	.012
.014	.020 wound
.008	.009
.024 wound	.026
.011	.012
.032	.036
.017	.020 plain
.040	.046
.022 wound	.026

MEDIUM	MEDIUM ELECTRIC
.011	.013
.011	.013
.015	.016
.015	.016
.024 W	.026
.010	.009
.030	.036
.014	.016
.042	.045
.022 W	.021W
.052	.056
.028	.030

PURE TUNING VERSUS EQUAL TEMPERAMENT

Many guitarists try to tune the guitar to pure chords (free of beats). These players have sensitive ears and prefer pure intervals and reject the mandatory equal temperament. They tune their guitar beautifully pure on the one chord only to discover that the next chord form is unacceptable. It is a problem of pure tuning versus equal temperament.

The guitar is an instrument of fixed pitch and the strings must be tuned to tempered intervals, not pure. Equal temperament is the name given to a system of dividing the chromatic scale into 12 equal half steps. Guitarists who have been trying to tune to one or another pure chord form must learn to understand and accept equal temperament. (Pure chords on all forms would require about three dozen frets within the octave.) But equal temperament reduces the number to twelve.

Try this, don't use harmonic tones at the 7th fret as a point of reference. Harmonic tones at the 7th fret are pure 5ths and in equal temperament each 5th must be lowered slightly.

But all harmonics at the 12th and 5th frets, being one and two octaves above the open strings, are immediately useful with this tuning technique. All octaves and unisons are pure on all instruments of fixed pitch. So use harmonics at 12th and 5th as reference tones in the following tuning instructions.

Tuning the 1st and 6th strings:

The E, open 1st string, must be in pure unison with the harmonic (see harmonic tuning) of the E, 6th string at the fifth fret. When these two strings have been tuned with each other, continue as follows.

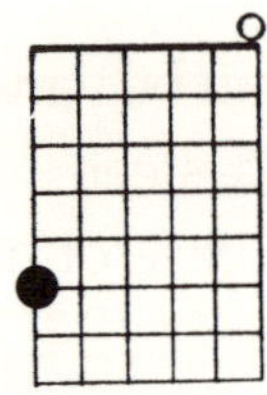

Tuning the 4th string:

Play a harmonic on the 6th string at the twelfth fret. As this sounds, tune the 4th string on the second fret until it is in pure unison with the 6th string.

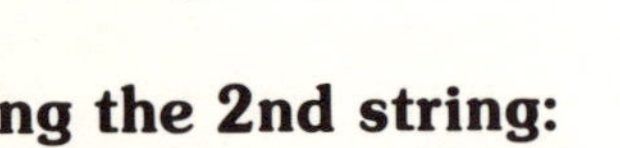
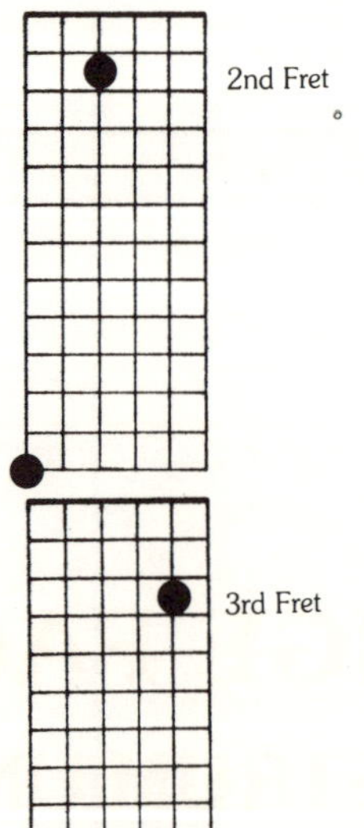

Tuning the 2nd string:

Play a harmonic on the 4th string at the twelfth fret. As this sounds, tune the 2nd string until D at the third fret is in pure unison with the 4th string.

Tuning the 3rd string:

Play a harmonic on the 4th string at the twelfth fret. As this sounds, tune the 3rd string until "D" at the 7th fret is in pure unison.

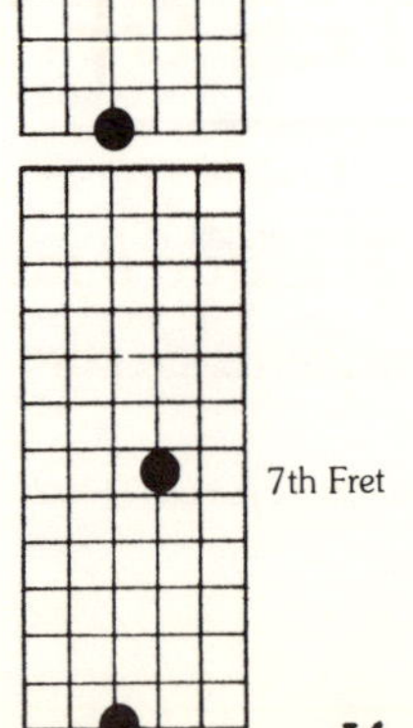

Make this check play a harmonic at the "G" string at the twelfth fret. As this sounds, play "G" on the 1st string at the third fret. The two tones should be in pure unison. If not, either you are at fault or the instrument does not fret true at the seventh fret. Go back and carefully check over each up to this point (check intonation). If the tones are still faulty, then readjust the 3rd string until the harmonic at the twelfth fret is in unison with the 1st string at the third fret. It is only the 3rd string we are trying to bring in tune. When the 1st, 6th, 4th, 2nd, and 3rd strings are in tune in that order continue with the 5th string.

Tuning the 5th string:

Play a harmonic on the 5th string at the twelfth fret. As this sounds, tune the 3rd string at the second fret until it is in pure unison with the 5th string.

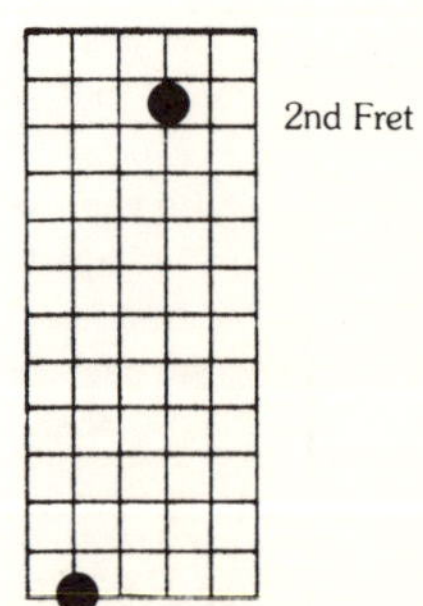

Now the strings will be tuned perfectly to equal temperament.

THE LAST ONE

1. Play a harmonic on the sixth (6) string at the 12th fret, as this sounds tune the 7th fret of the fifth (5) string. When these two strings have been tuned to each other, continue as follows.

2. Play a harmonic on the fifth (5) string at the 12th fret, as this sounds, tune the 7th fret of the fourth (4) string.

3. Play a harmonic on the fourth (4) string at the 12th fret, as this sounds, tune the 7th fret of the third (3) string.

4. Play a harmonic on the third (3) string at the 12th fret, as this sounds, tune the <u>8th fret</u> of the second (2) string.

5. Play a harmonic on the second (2) string at the 12th fret, as this sounds, tune the 7th fret of the first (1) string.

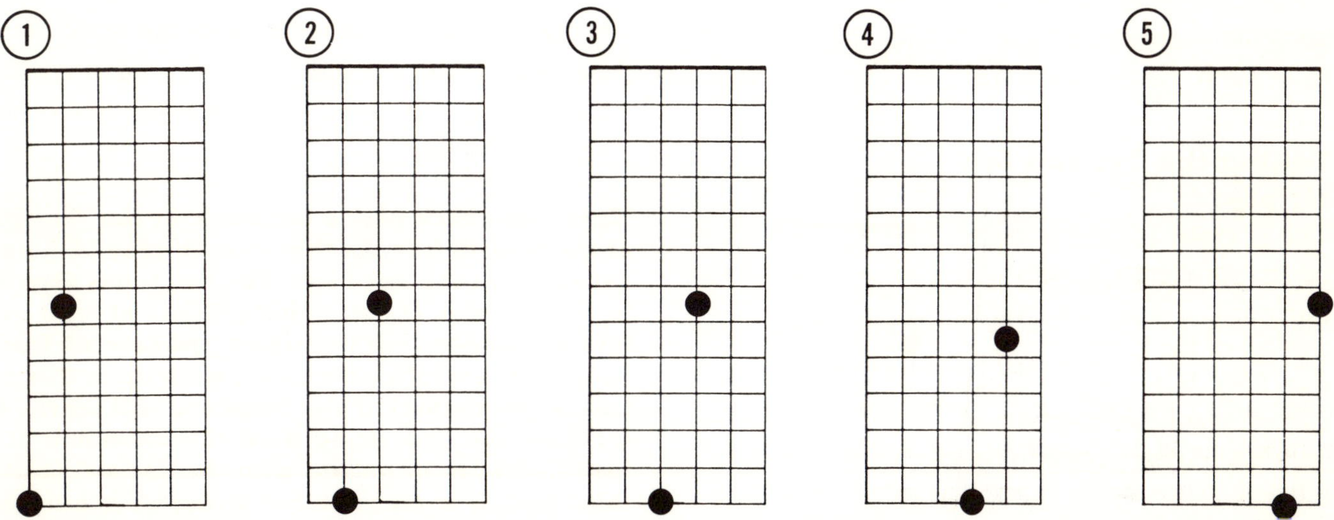

STRANGE FACT: #3

"DON'T STRUM UNTIL YOU SEE THE THE WHITES OF THEIR EYES!"

After they lost a battle to the Portuguese in the 1700's an army of Spaniards made a fast retreat to the hills. The victors, combing the battlefield for spoils, collected over 11,719 guitars.

CHANGING STRINGS

Sooner or later (sooner if you are just learning to tune your instrument) you'll have to change a string. It is a simple task, and take a few moments for each string. Here's a few guidelines to help.

FLAT-TOP ACOUSTIC GUITARS. The ball end of the string is placed into a hole in the bridge, and then the pin is inserted back into the hole. Some people think that bridge pins have to be hammered into place to hold the string securely. They don't. The proper method is to use the bridge pin to push the ball-end of the string into the hole. Once the ball has cleared the opening inside the guitar, it will slip to one side and you will be able to push the tapered bridge pin all the way down. As you do so, pull up gently on the string. The bridge pin only needs to be "finger-tight" to secure the string. The ball cannot come out of the hole since the bridge pin is in its way.

ARCH-TOP GUITARS and a few student-grade flat-top guitars have tailpieces to hold the ball-ends of the strings. You need only thread the string through the hole provided for it in the tailpiece, pulling it through until the ball-end stops against the metal of the tailpiece itself. Some tailpieces have notches.

ELECTRIC GUITARS AND BASS GUITARS The tailpiece will have notches or slits which you simply slide the ball-end of the string into the appropriate notch. Just be careful that the ball doesn't slip out of the notch while you are bringing the string up to pitch.

CLASSIC GUITARS Some nylon strings have ball-ends — these are simply run through the bridge holes. The ones that don't are a little harder, you insert the string through the hole in bridge, saddle side first and form a loop as shown below and then tighten.

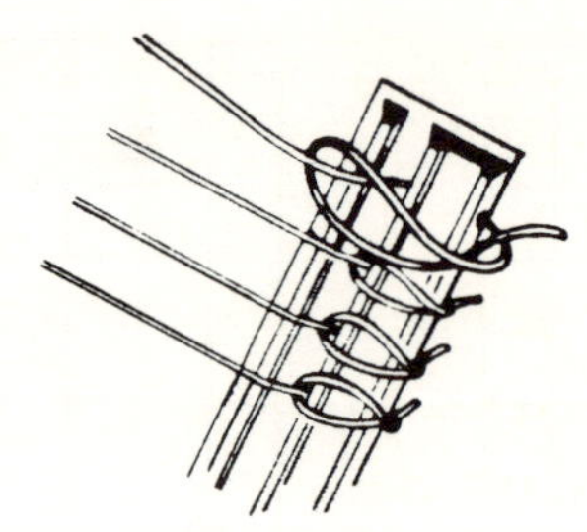

ATTACHING STRINGS TO TUNING POST. (Machine Heads, Tuning Keys)

Thread the string through the hole into the post, then pass it *under* the rest of the string where it was inserted into the hole, and *back over* in the opposite direction. Crimp this "fold" so it locks the string in place, and slowly bring the string up to pitch. The *tuned* string should run completely around the post one to three times. A unwound string, particularly a light gauge one, may need to go through the hole a second time to guard against slippage. A wound string will only need to go through the hole once and then be bent in the opposite direction.

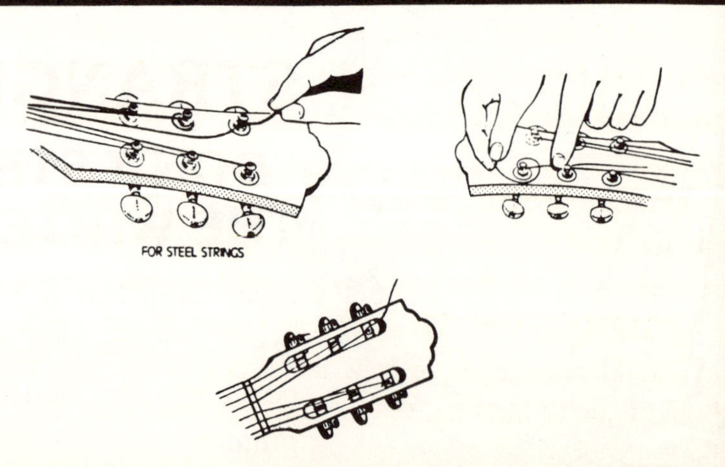

PICKY, PICKY, PICKY

ALL ABOUT PICKS

Although guitar picks don't make your guitar out of tune there are a few things we could say about them, other than the fact that trying to get a pick from the inside of an acoustic guitar is a maddening experience or trying to find one that just dropped from your hand that you know should be right at your feet . . . after what seems like hours of searching (it's your favorite pick) you find it clear across the room. Really, all picks are different and some will sound better than others.

Selecting the right pick is a subjective matter, what follows is just some information. I suggest trying several kinds until you find the right one that suits you.

SHAPE: Think of a shape, any kind of shape, and chances are someone made a pick like it. The standard shape is the triangle with the point slightly dulled and its base points rounded. Other shapes: the tear-drop, is a triangular flat pick (an equilateral triangle with three identically pointed or slightly rounded corners). There's heart shaped too, a triangle pick with the three corners of different shapes and thickness. The thumb pick (basically a flat pick), curved to fit over the thumb. And the finger pick that fits over the ends of your fingers, used mostly with the thumb pick. Note: A round-tipped pick will glide off the guitar string more readily than a pointed-tipped pick. So a round-tipped pick will give you a mellower tone and a pointed tip should give you a cleaner, more defined sound.

SIZE: There are three pick sizes; 1 small, 2 medium and large. **Small** heavier gauged picks (a favorite of Jazz players) will allow greater control than a large flimsy pick. Small picks vary in length. **Medium** picks are fairly uniform. The Fender or Gibson medium gauge has become the standard of picks as its good for all types of styles. **Large** picks are just large and a bit hard to play as you can loose control and accuracy.

MATERIAL: The pick has been around for centuries some of the early picks were made of bone, tortoise shell, ivory and stone. They are still made today, the turtle shell pick has the nice advantage of being thin and still rigid. Turtles don't like giving up their home for us guitar pickers, so they're getting hard to find. Bone is fairly hard but not as durable as ivory or stone. A stone pick is highly polished, made from agate (it's expensive too). One advantage of a stone pick is its resistance to string wear. A disadvantage: don't drop it. Synthetic picks: metal flat picks are used a lot by hard-rock players, it gives a raspy, percussive sound. Unfortunately it likes to eat up the strings and can cause them to unwind. Plastic and nylon picks are the most common today. The nylon pick is durable and will not readily break or chip. They cost more than the plastic pick, which is the most popular. The plastic picks break the easiest and wear out the fastest. Felt picks, a felt pick is supposed to sound like playing the bass with your fingers. I've never seen anyone use a felt pick. The 'whatever' pick: as a last resort use whatever is handy, cardboard matchbook covers, a quarter, toothpick, those little plastic square things they put on the end of bread wrappers, etc.

THICKNESS: Thickness or gauge is a key point. The "thin," "medium" and "heavy" are the ones you see most. For the most part a thin pick will make a brushy, slappy noise when strumming. A medium or heavy pick will give you more control of attack, more volume and less sloppiness.

HOLDING ON: When you first learn to use a pick, the plain-surfaced pick has a tendency to slip around. Manufacturers came to the rescue. Some picks have cork at the base and other picks have a hole in the center of the base to give you skin to skin contact, and others have designed grid-like surfaces on the picks base. All good ideas, try one.

Now with all this knowledge you can be a very picky person.

DEFINING INTONATION

Proper intonation is the concept that your guitar should be in tune with itself throughout the various playing ranges; meaning from chord to chord in various positions, from key to key, and scale to scale, all tones will interrelate harmoniously.

If you have to make slight tuning adjustments when you change keys, like going from E to D or when you play up and down the neck and certain chords or notes sound out of tune, your guitar may be **out of tune with itself.**

Another test is whether the note pressed at the 12th fret of each string is sharp or flat in relation to the harmonic played over the same fret on that string.

WHAT CAUSES INTONATION: Some factors are string gauge, false or damaged strings, truss rod adjustment, action height at bridge and nut and string length. Of these, action height and string length are the most important. The methods of adjusting, modifying or regulating these factors vary with the types of guitar (electrics, basses, acoustics or classicals).

On electric guitars and basses the bridge will have adjustment screws making string length adjustments relatively easy. On acoustics and classics the bridge and saddle are fixed in place so adjusting string length is more difficult.

Incorrect fret location would cause intonation problems by establishing intervals that do not conform to the equal tempered scale. Luckily most finger boards are slotted accurately by machine.

Change strings check intonation. Remember string type (gauge and alloy), action height in combination with string length are the critical points of intonation. If any of these are changed, check intonation. Every guitar is different. Some will stay in tune with themselves for long periods of time, others will go out of tune (intonation) quickly.

NECK WARP: The neck or fingerboard is supposed to have a very slight amount of warp between the nut and the spot where the neck joins the body. This is so that when a string is pressed and picked it will vibrate without striking the other frets. (The bridge height alone is not high enough to cause free movement of the string at positions below the spot where the neck joins the body.) Excessive warp has a sharping effect because the string must travel an extra distance to reach the fingerboard.

HOW TO TEST THE AMOUNT OF WARP: Press down a string simultaneously at the first fret and at the fret where the neck joins the body. If you see more than 1/32 of an inch the neck has excessive warp. If no space, there is a counter-warp, and warp must be added. See your guitar repairman.

BRIDGE ADJUSTMENTS FOR ACOUSTICS AND CLASSICS
(Action Height)

Again use the gauge and type of strings you will be using, tuned to playing pitch. The strings affect action height by stressing the neck.

Sight along the neck from the bridge and be sure that the saddle conforms to the curve or flatness of the fingerboard. If it doesn't, remove the saddle and shape it's curvature to conform to that of the fingerboard. **Work slowly and carefully** with a fret or mill file.

The **rounded** saddle (Fig. 1) is used most for steel-string acoustic. The **beveled** saddle (Fig. 2) for classical guitars. If you use a rounded shape for classical the string windings vibrate against it, causing buzzing.

After correcting the saddle curvature, reinsert the saddle.

Some players like lower or higher action but the ideal height for acoustic steel-string guitar is with the sixth string at 3/32" and the first string at 2/32". Classical guitars; sixth at 4/32" and first at 3/32". These measurements are taken at the fret where the neck joins the body. (The other strings will automatically arrive at appropriate heights when the first and sixth are set.)

THUMB RULE: If you lower a string by a certain amount you must remove approximately twice that amount from the saddle.

Take the saddle out of the bridge (Fig. 3), measure off and mark each end (sixth and first string) and draw a line between these points, grind down the saddle to that line (sandpaper or mill file). Put back the saddle and retune the strings and check the measurements again. Work slowly and cautiously. It's easy to remove material but difficult to replace it. If you cut too much off the saddle most music stores carry replacements.

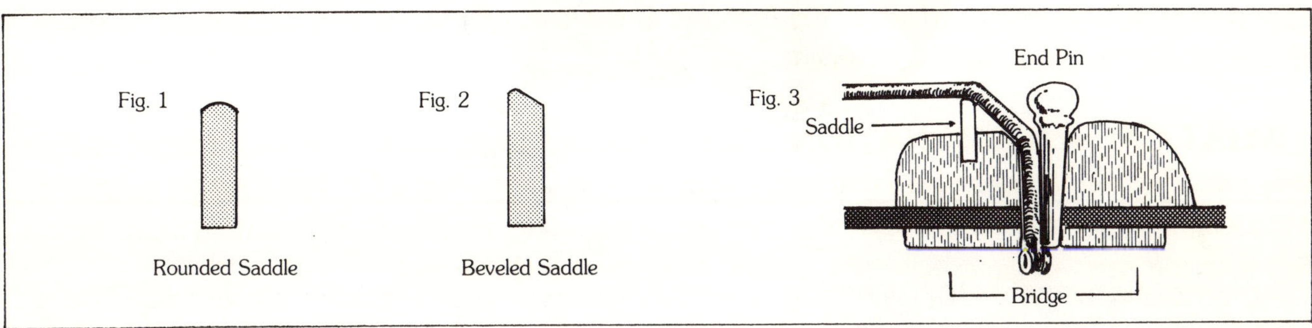

BRIDGE ADJUSTMENTS FOR ELECTRICS: You'll need a small screwdriver or allen wrenches.

The same thumb rule should apply for electrics and basses, but since the adjustment is done mechanically, it is unnecessary to consider raising or lowering the saddle twice the height.

For electrics and basses you just take the initial measurement and raise or lower the saddle height adjustment screws (Fig. 4) until the desired measurement is achieved. For basses the recommended action height is 4/32" forth string, 3/32" first string, that's a low setting, higher action would be 5/32" forth string, 4/32" first string. Remember, that's at the fret where the neck joins the body.

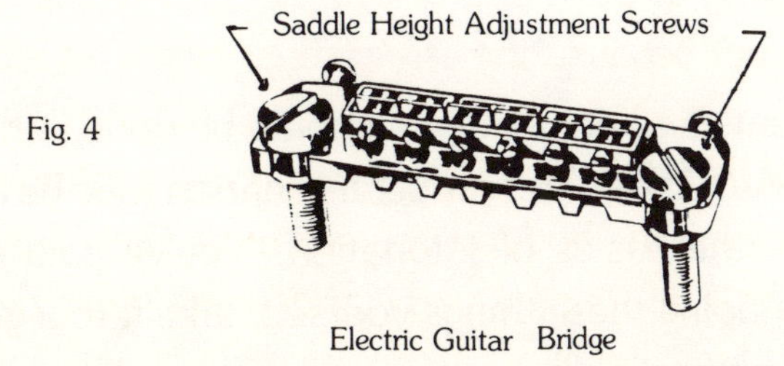

ADJUSTING STRING LENGTH ON ELECTRICS AT THE BRIDGE: Remember to use the type of strings that you will use regularly. Leave **new** strings on a few hours at full tension before you adjust the length. Most electric guitars and basses have the same type of bridge that you can adjust each strings saddle (Fig. 5) forward or backward to alter string length. You'll need a small screwdriver, phillips screwdriver or allen wrench for the screw heads. One direction of turning the screw will move the saddle forward toward the neck to compensate for flatness. The opposite direction to compensate for sharpness. Using an electronic tuning device (see electronic tuning section) to test harmonics and their corresponding notes at the 12th fret, it is possible to set string length accurately. Note: changing the make or gauge of the strings later on will probably effect your intonation and you'll have to reset the lengths again.

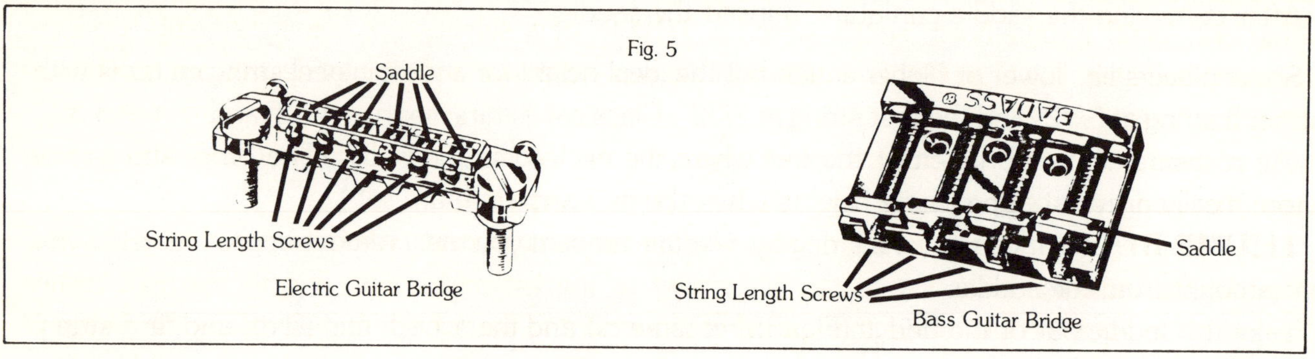

ADJUSTING ACTION AT THE NUT: (Fig. 6). We've talked about adjusting the action at the bridge, now we'll discuss height adjustments at the nut. As usual use the strings and the gauge you'll be using, tuned to playing pitch.

Use a mechanic's feeler gauge that measures widths of at least between .020" and .026". Hold the gauge parallel to the string surface at the first fret. Between the first fret and the bottom of **each** string is where you take the measurement.

Steel String Acoustic — .022"
Classical Guitar — .022" to .026"
Electric Guitars — .020"
Bass Guitars — .022"

These measurements are high enough to avoid buzzing and low enough to be comfortable. Lower or higher setting can be used if you like. (All the measurements given are only basic guidelines.) If the string is too high, you slot the nut deeper and remeasure until the gauge touches both fret and string. (Use a fine-tooth hacksaw blade or X-Acto saw.) Go very slow, cut a small amount and then remeasure. Remember to bring the string to its full pitch as you remeasure.

If the slot is too deep or you cut more than you intended to, the nut may have to be shimmed or replaced.

SUMMARY: The measurements and adjustments should be done in this order: 1) truss rod; 2) action height; 3) string length. If done out of order proper intonation may be achieved in one step only to be lost in another. This covers the basics of intonation. You've paid a lot of money for your instrument, if you're not sure about doing these things yourself, take it to a guitar repairman. He's the expert and has a high degree of technical skill.

ELECTRONIC TUNING DEVICES

Why use an electronic tuning device? It's not really necessary, but tuning devices are far more accurate than the human ear because they 1) register **only** the actual pitch of the note; 2) they can "hear" much smaller frequency changes and 3) are consistent indexes of relative and absolute pitch. There are several types of electronic tuning devices which can be used to tune with. Some of the methods are the stroboscopic meter, cathode tube and light pulsation. The stroboscopic devices are usually accurate to within one "cent" (pronounced "sont"), which is 1/100th of a semitone, a semitone being a normal chromatic half-step, like G to G#. Even some of the less expensive and simpler devices are accurate to within five "cents."

All of them work on the basic concept of translating the incoming signal (musical note) into a visual image that correctly shows whether the note is on pitch, sharp or flat.

HOW THEY WORK: Most tuning devices work in the same manner, when the note being played is on pitch, the indicator holds on center. Movement to the left means flat, and to the right means sharpness. On stroboscopic tuners the **speed** of movement to the right or the left means the degree of sharpness or flatness.

The range of products on the market is wide and varied, both in price and function. Most tuners show their readings in cents deviation from the tones of the equally tempered scale based on the American pitch A of 440 cycles/sec., or hertz (hz). Deviations are tones sharper than standard and minus deviations are tones flatter than standard.

All tuners do the same job but the way they get their results is slightly different.

Here we look at some of the tuners available.

KORG GT-6

Compact and lightweight, designed expressly for guitar and bass, features a six-position note selector switch and a meter with built in lamp for viewing in the dark. Has an instrument input jack and an output or "amp" jack so you can listen to the guitar while tuning. Plus built-in mike for acoustic guitars. Battery powered.

ZEN-ON JUSTINA

One of the smallest tuners on the market uses an easy to read meter to show whether the note is sharp or flat. Covers only the six guitar notes, plus built-in mike for acoustic guitar. Battery powered.

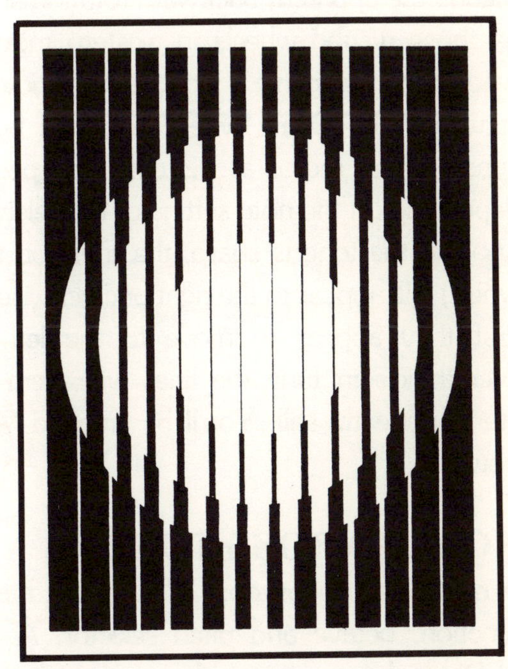

OVATION'S "THE TUNER"

Has a stroboscopic light source specially designed for visually tuning both electric and acoustic plus other fretted instruments like five string banjo and 12-string guitars. This unit is placed **directly over the neck of the guitar**. (After you've preset the selector knob to the open string you want to tune.) When you pick the string you'll see a vibrating image if its out of tune. As you adjust the string to proper pitch, the movement will slow down. When properly tuned it will be motionless. Easy to use. Battery powered.

PETERSON 420

Claims an accuracy of 1/3 cent. Has a range of eight octaves, enough to tune a piano. Has a built-in mike for acoustics. Works on the strobe disc system. AC powered. This tuner would be enough to keep a whole band in tune for an entire record contract.

CONN STROBOTUNER MODEL ST-11

This tuning device works on an optical illusion known as the **stroboscopic** effect. Means the apparent backward rotation such as those wagon wheels in western movies when the wagon is obviously moving forward. The Conn "wheel" is driven by a synchronous motor at 12 different speeds depending on the note setting of the selector knob. If the tone is sharp, the lines (on the wheel) will appear to the right or clockwise, if first they appear to move to the left. If everything's in tune the lines will seem to stand perfectly still. You'll be amazed. AC powered.

ROLAND BOSS TU-120

A neat little stroboscopic 12 note unit, has a function, octave and pitch selector. A 16 LED display, built-in mike, calibrator and monitor. Operates on batteries or AC. Ideal for all types of instruments. Electric instruments are plugged in. Tunes over five octave range.

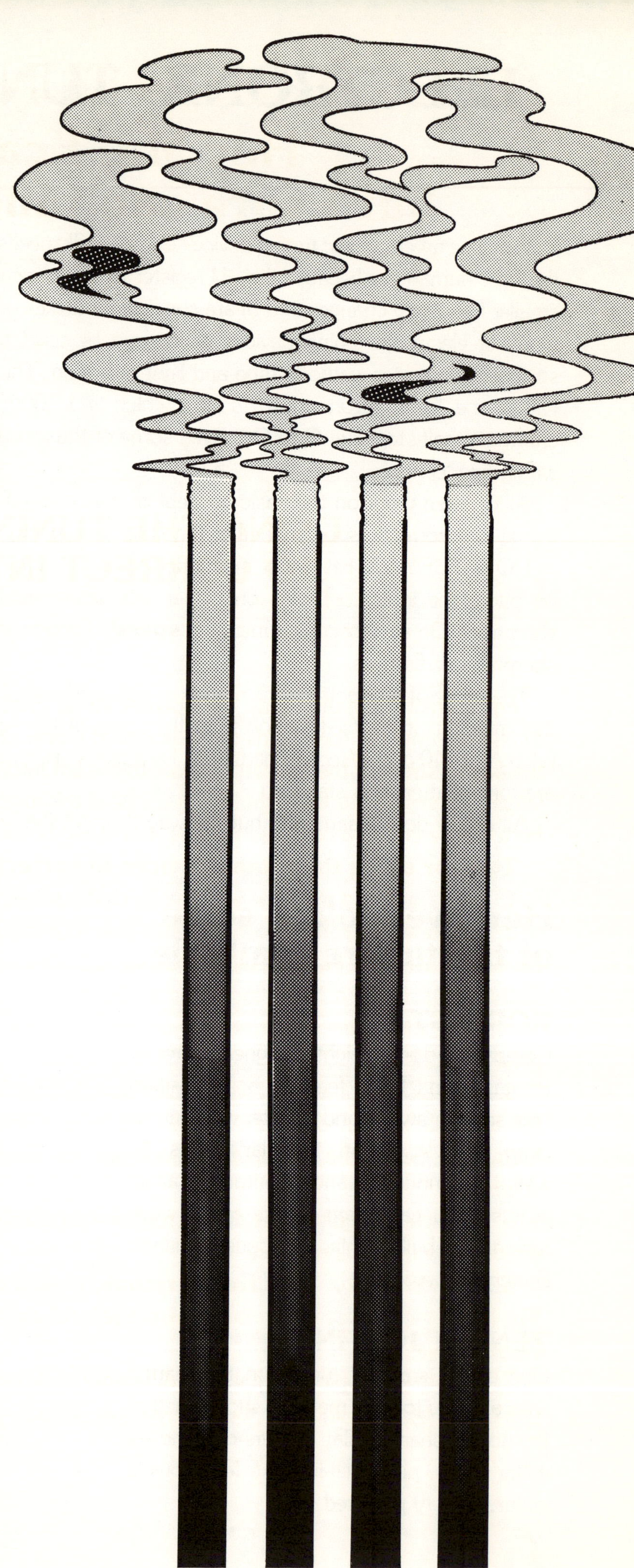

"Hey Ma, I can't read, but I sure can tune my guitar."

USING THE TUNING DEVICES TO CORRECT INTONATION

For correct intonation play the open A string (5th) **harmonic** at the 12th fret and adjust the tuning key until the tone holds the indicator at center. Then play the **fretted** note at the 12th fret of the **same** string. If the indicator moves to the left intonation is flat, and you must shorten the string length. Movement to the right and you'll need to lengthen the string. When both the harmonic and fretted note create a centered reading, the string is correctly intonated.

Tips for using the tuning devices to correct intonation:

1. Make sure the machine is correctly calibrated in accordance with its instruction manual.

2. Pre-tune the guitar to concert pitch (use a tuning fork to get the correct pitch). It's necessary to have full tension on the neck when making adjustments. Also the string which is not tuned to correct pitch may give you a false reading on a strobe.

3. Hold the guitar in normal playing position when testing. Testing this way compensates for playing conditions.

4. For electric guitars and basses plug directly into the tuning device. Then set the tone controls at full treble to get an optimum signal, and tune a given string to the device (using the 12th fret harmonic). Select the pickup that gives you the clearest reading. Also experiment with levels of volume.

5. For acoustic guitars use the microphone supplied with the unit. Or use a contact pick-up to plug directly into the tuning device.

6. Always use the **12th fret harmonic** instead of the open string when tuning to the device. The harmonic creates more vibrations per second, causing a more continuous signal and therefore a clearer image.

7. On stroboscopic machines the different bands on the strobe dial are for different octaves. And one of the bands will be for the note you are testing.

STRING SMARTS
WHAT YOU SHOULD KNOW

The principle behind the musical string is an ageless phenomenon of physics and not an "invention." A tightened cord, when struck or plucked, will continue to vibrate until its energy is exhausted. As it vibrates, it will cause the air around it to move. If it is attached to a membrane such as a guitar soundboard, larger masses of wir will move. Or the vibrating string might pass over an electromagnetic pickup which will begin the process to energize a speaker cone to move large masses of air. That air movement translates into waves of sound pressure which carry to our ears and trigger the amazing biomechanical processes we call our sense of hearing.

The famous Greek mathematician/philosopher Pythagoras (who died about 497 B.C.) laid the foundation for modern acoustical physics, and his theories about string vibration have held up for 2,500 years. With the benefit of modern scientific analysis, however, we have a better understanding of the way strings work.

THE PHYSICS OF THE MUSICAL STRING

This text is not intended to be an in-depth study of musical acoustics, but there are some terms that are used which you should be familiar with. Here is a preview:

Fundamental — The lowest note a string can produce at a specific tension; the string's lowest rate of vibration.

Vibration — The back-and-forth movement of an object; in this case, a musical string.

Mode — The pattern or patterns of a musical string's vibrations.

Partials — A term used to number and organize the various modes of a string's vibrations. The fundamental is the 1st partial; the next mode is the 2nd partial (a full description follows in the text); and so on.

Harmonics — Sounds made by plucking a string and then touching it as various points along its length to force it to vibrate in specific modes.

Overtones — Basically the same as harmonics, but the word is used to describe the quality that the harmonics impart to the total sound of the string when it is played.

A plucked string doesn't "twang" around in a series of random movements; it vibrates in a specific and generally predictable pattern. The string actually vibrates in a number of segments, called "modes." The most basic mode is called the "fundamental" — the lowest possible rate at which, relative to its particular tension, the string can vibrate. That model, illustrated in Fig. 1, involves the entire length of the string vibrating in a complete back-and-forth motion.

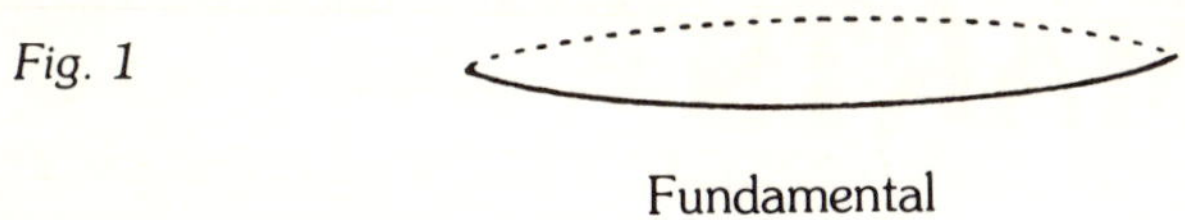

Fig. 1

Fundamental

The fundamental is also the term we use to designate the open (unfretted) *note* produced by the string when tuned to its intended pitch. If you slacken the tension, you lower the fundamental (open string pitch), and if you increase the tension, you raise the fundamental.

If we take a string and tighten it to a point such that in one second it makes 440 complete back-and-forth vibrations, we will have an A string. Measuring the vibrations gives us a useful mathematical handle on the interesting things that happen when a string is plucked. There is more going on than the full back-and-forth motion. The string vibrates in individual parts as well, and these individual vibrations, called partials, have a specific order. Let's study some of them, using the fundamental as a starting point. The fundamental is called the 1st partial. The second mode, or 2nd partial, is illustrated in Fig. 2.

Fig. 2

First Overtone Second Tonic

When the string is plucked, it also begins to vibrate in two segments, or halves — interspersing those half-segment motions with full-length motions. The half-segments of the string vibrate *twice* as fast as the full string, and this produces a note which is one octave higher than the fundamental. These modes are called partials because they are produced by *part* of the string, and they form *part* of the overall sound.

If you pluck a string tuned to A 440, then a harmonk at the 12th fret, you'll hear the A 880, and the A 440 will be cancelled. Why? The 12th fret is the midpoint of the string's length. By touching the string there, you cancel out or "damp" the full-length vibration and cause a "node" or nonvibrating point to occur in the center of the string. What remains in the vibration of the string in two halves: the 2nd partial.

There are quite a few partials for any given note — up to 16 or 18.

Besides vibrating in halves, a string vibrates in thirds. Touch that a 440 string at either the 7th fret or the 19th fret — the points that divide the string into thirds — and you'll hear the note E 1320Hz. That is the 3rd partial as seen in Fig. 3.

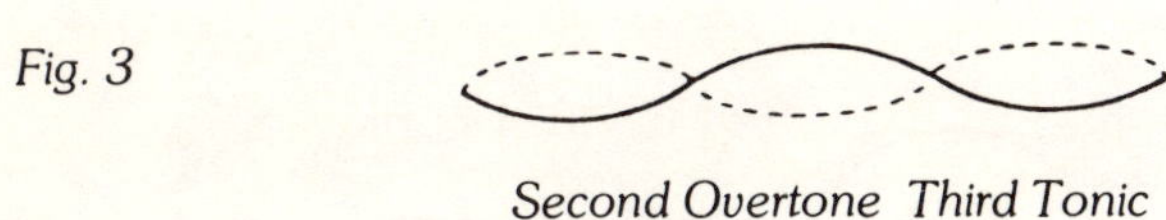

Fig. 3

Second Overtone Third Tonic

Following the laws of physics, those one-third segments are each vibrating three times faster than the full string. Three times 440Hz equals 1,320Hz. Likewise, the 4th partial is 1,Z60Hz, or four times 440Hz. The 5th partial is 2,200Hz or five times 440Hz, etc.

STRING GAUGE …………

A gauge is the measurement of the string's thickness given in thousandths of an inch, millimeters, or both (as a cross-reference).

Some instruments sound better when fitted with a particular gauge and type of string. Some gauges and types of strings reproduce better electronically than others. And, the lighter gauge strings are easier to play than heavier gauge strings.

A THIN string will vibrate faster than a THICK one when both are at the same tension. Light strings can move more rapidly, and faster vibration rates produce higher tones.

MASS

Mass affects pitch. As the mass (size and weight) of a string increases, the rate at which it is able to vibrate decreases. Low-note strings don't need to vibrate as fast as high-note strings and by weighting them down, they decrease in speed. The trick is to give low-rate strings the right amount of mass without making them hard to play.

String engineers solve the problem by using a technique that was pioneered over three centuries ago. A thin core wire is carefully spun with a second (and sometimes a third) wrap wire, producing a string with the mass of two wires, yet with most of the flexibility of a single wire.

Many combinations of wire gauges can be combined to achieve the same overall string diameter. Fig. 4 shows three core-and-wrap combinations, each making up a .054" (fifty-four thousandths) string. Each of the combinations shown in Fig. 4 could produce an acceptable low E string for a guitar; but each will have different characteristics of sound and playing "feel".

THE LONG STRETCH

Strings stretch much like a rubber band: they are elastic to a point, but after reaching that point, they have virtually no elasticity left. Stretched too far, they have a "cold", "thin", sound and are so close to the rupture point that their useful life is minimal. For a .009" high E string on a guitar with a 25.5" string scale length, for example, the rupture point is reached when the string is stretched approximately .195" beyond its original length. Tuning that string up to pitch only stretches it about .135".

TENSION IN THE LIVES OF STRINGS

The amount of tension that each string requires is a very important aspect of musical string design and selection. For example, several different gauges of plain strings can be chosen for the guitar's high E string. When brought to the same pitch (E), each increasing gauge (thickness of wire) will be relatively stiffer and exert relatively greater tension. Aside from affecting the playing "feel" of the string, the tension is also important to the physics of the instrument. On acoustic instruments the string's tension "loads" the soundboard and prepares it to be sensitive to the string's vibrations. On instruments with electro-magnetic pickups, the tension is more important to the flexibility of the string and defines the string's path over the pickup.

Keep these four viewpoints in mind:
1. **The overall mass of the string.**
2. **The relationship**
3. **The stretch factor at each gauge.**
4. **The specific tension each string has when brough to pitch.**

From these factors, a reliable range of string gauges has been established over the years to satisfy the most discriminating musicians.

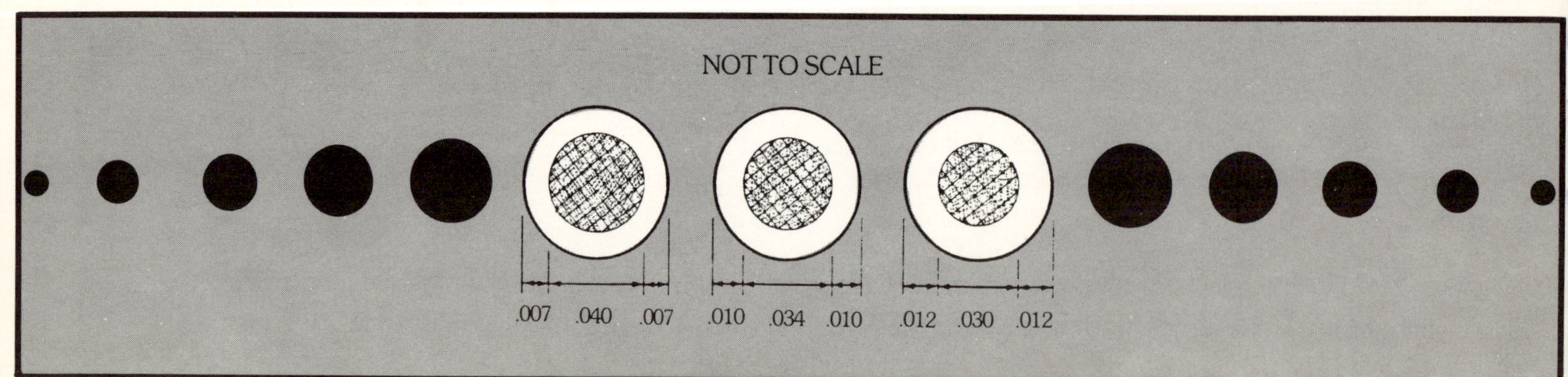

FINDING THE RIGHT STRING FOR YOU

In the 1981 Gibson string catalog you'll find load graph's as a means of evaluating the merits of an individual string or set by determining the tension or "load" that each string presents when tuned to pitch. Each string instrument family has particular loading requirements with respect to string tension (of course, gauges are included as a standard of reference). Check it out, it will really help.

THE LOADED GUITAR
Each Instrument Has a Special Need

ACOUSTIC FLAT-TOP GUITAR'S soundboard is loaded when all of its strings are brought up to pitch. The soundboard is torqued (twisted) into playing position by the pull of the strings. When a string is plucked, there is a direct interaction between the force of string and the counterforce presented by the soundboard; the soundboard wants to return to its original shape and the string's tension wants to pull it further (and release it as well).

Some soundboards are stiff and require higher load levels to activate them, while others are limber and require lower load levels. If you have a guitar that sounds strong on every string except its middle two or three strings, you can select a set of strings that offers those few strings with higher loads. The increased tension on those strings will usually improve the characteristics of the overall sound.

ARCH-TOP GUITARS, both electric and acoustic, experience a different loading force than their flat-top cousins. While flat-top guitars have a fixed bridge in the middle of the soundboard, arch-top guitars have their strings secured by a tailpiece. The strings then pass *over* the bridge. Because of this feature, the instrument's lengthwise (longitudinal) load is secondary to its downward (lateral) load. The string's force is directed *downward,* through the bridge, to the soundboard, instead of torquing or twisting the bridge as on flat-top instruments. Likewise, the soundboard, pushes back and meets the bridge with equal resistance. Most arch-tops have bridges with two adjustable screw posts. The outer strings, crossing the bridge near the posts, provide different tonal characteristics than the inner strings, which are farther from the posts and therefore don't transmit their vibrations to the soundboard as directly. To counteract this tendency, you would choose a set of strings with higher loads on the center strings and lower loads on the other strings.

SOLID BODY GUITARS. The loading force on the soundboard of solid body electric guitars is much less important than it is on acoustic stringed instruments since the soundboard, as such, is non-existent.

The important consideration for solid body instruments is to achieve good string-to-string balance, so that the strings all move in a similar way within the magnetic field of the pickup or pickups. Thus from a standpoint of tension, the loading is an important aspect of the strength of each string's vibrational pattern and how each string will relate to the pickup. String sets with higher loads on various strings should be selected where more "cut" or "drive" is needed on those strings to compensate for electronic difficiencies, or for the player's preferences.

A typical load graph illustration as it appears in the Gibson String catalog.

ELECTRIC
G-740L ROCK & ROLL
Nickel Plated Steel

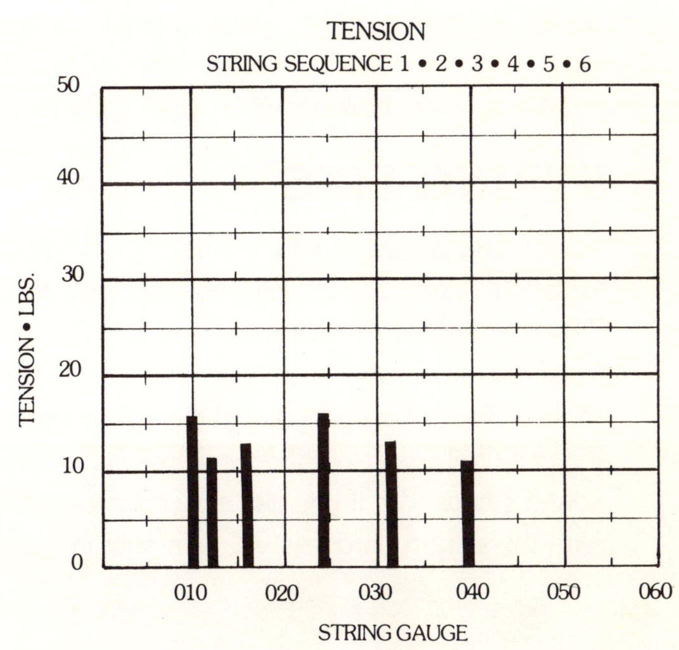

TUNING	GAUGES IN	MM
E-1st p	.010	.254
B-2nd p	.012	.305
G-3rd p	.016	.406
D-4th w	.024	.610
A-5th w	.032	.813
E-6th w	.039	.991

WINDINGS, ROUND AND FLAT

To smooth out the feel for the heavier strings of electric guitars and electric bases, and to eliminate finger squeaks, a series of flat windings were developed. Flat-wound strings are achieved in two basic ways. The simplest is to actually wind a flat ribbon-like string around the core wire. The second, is to wind a round wire onto the core, then grind half of it away, leaving a flattened surface. The grinding process is followed by a special polishing step to assure a bright smooth playing surface.

Because the ground-flat strings are round on their undersides, they are a big more flexible than true flat-wound strings. The flexibility provides more harmonics (partials) and ground-wound (or half-flat) strings tend to be brighter and richer than the true flat-wound strings. Compound strings provide substantial mass for a low pitch; especially important for the jazz guitarist and the electric bass player.

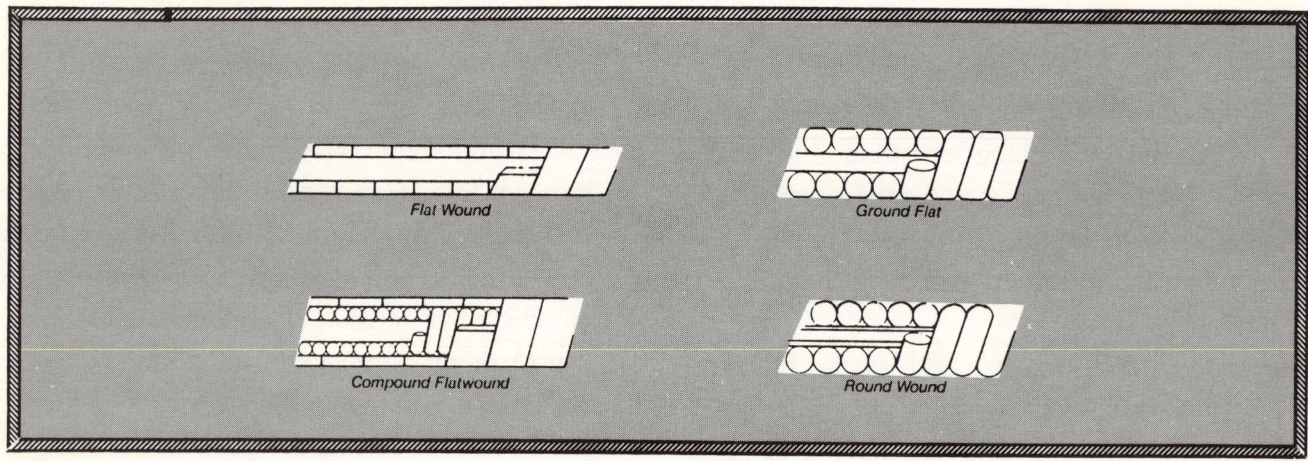

NEW STRINGS

Strings are elastic. They stretch. This gradual process eventually leads to "dead" sounding strings. Strings do most of their stretching when you first install them. They will sound exceptionally bright and metallic for the first 24 hours or so; then (in most cases) they will maintain good tonal characteristics for the next four to six weeks. Afterwards, they slowly give up their remaining elasticity and the string's tone quality diminishes. Hard, constant playing will also shorten that "four-to-six-week" period.

STRING LIFE

Very fine grades of wire are used for musical instrument strings, but the metal is still susceptible to oxidation. After playing the instrument, it's a good idea to regularly wipe off the strings with a cleaner like Gibson's "Grit Gone." Windings tend to collect dirt and mositure, and the presence of foreign matter with the string's structure doesn't promote good sound. Keep a wipe cloth in your instrument case and use it on the strings whenever you put the instrument away. Some "heavy fretters" can be very tough on strings and can easily wear out the windings on the softer alloys such as silver-plated copper. Change to brass-wound strings. Or, if you like nickel-plated steel, but wear out the windings, move up to stainless steel. With the shift in hardness will be a shift in tone. You will have to give up one quality to get another.

STRING MATERIALS And Tone Color

Loading, winding and elasticity all affect the performance of musical strings. The materials of the strings are made of are also important affecting another dimension of string performance: tone color. Each family of metals has its own tonal characteristics due to the inherent differences in springiness, mass, or both. What follows is a list of the different types of strings.

BRONZE-WOUND STRINGS are a favorite of acoustic players because of their bright, focused sound. They feature a brisk ringing attack, good sustain. They are bright and brassy when you want them to be, with a clear, penetrating tone.

BRASS-WOUND STRINGS equally as popular with acoustic players as bronze-wound, have a very bright, full-bodied tone with good depth. Brass-wound strings are neither as bright as bronze, nor as mellow as silver-plated copper. The decay rate is slower than silver-plated copper and nickel-plated steel-wound strings, providing a longer ring to harmonics. Heavy, louder, and brighter, brass-wound strings meet the requirements of flatpickers and energetic fingerpickers alike.

MONEL-WOUND STRINGS have a darker, fuller tone than either stainless steel-wound or nickel-plated steel-wound strings and are not as billiant as bronze or brass. Monel offers a mellower attack and a more gradual peak and decay. These strings lend themselves to lead playing and jazz chording. The "feel" is a little coarser than that of the bronze and silver plated varieties. Monel is a very durable alloy and can withstand lots of hard playing and heavy left-hand fretting.

SILVER-PLATED COPPER-WOUND STRINGS have a delicate, transparent sound, with a crisp, penetrating attack. By comparison to bronze-wound strings, silver-plated copper has a rounder, warmer tone. The decay rate is somewhat faster than that of most other string materials. Silver-plated copper offers a nice compromise between nylon and bronze and are good finger-picking strings for folk players.

SILK AND STEEL STRINGS (silver-plated-copper wound) are made of an unusual and often overlooked combination of materials. This set offers the driving force of steel strings and the soft tonal (mellowness) properties associated with classical strings. The steel cores provide this set with the energy needed to drive an acoustic guitar's soundboard. Around the core wire (on the four wound strings) is a filament covering of silk fiber which increases the mass, provides a soft feel, and *minimizes* the brilliance. This set is the perfect choice for the folk guitarist, or for the beginner's delicate fingers.

BRONZE-WOUND STRINGS are for use on the lightly-braced classical guitars. The three bass strings are made of a multifilament nylon-strand core covered with a special bronze wrap-wire. The three plain strings in the classical sets are made of a high-density monofilament nylon engineered to provide the rich timbre associated with the classical sound.

NICKEL-WOUND STRINGS are chosen by electric and acoustic guitar players alike. Nickel offers a sound that is darker, rounder and fuller than that of bronze strings (for acoustic materials) and nickel-plated or stainless (for electric guitars). Sustain is comparatively shorter than that of bronze and stainless but projects crispness and brightness, with abundant consonant overtones.

NICKEL-PLATED STEEL-WOUND STRINGS are the "hot" strings preferred by so many of the rock guitarists. They have a brighter sound and more "punch" than pure nickel-wound strings. The extra light sets are smooth and easy — almost approaching the feel of flat-wound strings. Notes peak fast, hold steady, then decay quickly, with a resulting good tonal definition. The nickel-plating contributes to the tonal characteristics and also provides a silvery nontarnishing surface for the steel.

STAINLESS STEEL-WOUND STRINGS have a brilliant tone, evoking some of the "ringing" attack qualities of bronze strings, but used primarily by electric guitarists. They have a "majestic" tone and are neither too bright nor too mellow. There is a metallic warmth coupled with a forceful but not sharp tone. Stainless steel-wound strings are very durable and, of course, resist tarnish.

MATERIALS	Guitar (Arch-top)	Guitar (Flat-top)	Guitar (Classical)	Acoustic Guitar (Piezo/Transducer)	Acoustic Guitar (magnetic coil)	Solid Body Guitar (magnetic coil)	Bass (magnetic coil)
Bronze		X		X			
Brass		X		X			
Monel	X			X	X	X	
Silver-plated copper	X	X		X			
Silk and steel		X		X			
Nylon.			X				
Nickel	X			X	X	X	X
Nickel-plated steel	X			X	X	X	X
Stainless	X	X		X	X	X	X

SOME COMMON STRING QUESTIONS

Q: Are bronze strings better than steel strings for acoustic guitar?
A: None are "better" than the others. It is a matter of personal preference.

Q: I have a buzz on my lower strings, but my action is pretty high. What can be done?
A: A wrap can come loose from hard playing. It will break or fracture against the fret and can go completely unnoticed because the break is under the string, between the string and the fret. A loose winding will often cause buzzes. Change strings.

Q: I have a buzz and my action is just right. What causes this?
A: This is common on new strings for the first day or so. If the wraps are not loose or broken and the strings are at least two weeks old, you have have a problem not related to strings (such as some high frets) and you should have your guitar checked by a repairperson.

Q: How often should I change strings?
A: If you want the instrument to sound bright and full, and you are playing about an hour a day, you should change strings about once every eight or ten weeks.

Q: should I put new strings on before every gig?
A: No, if you change them just before each gig, you will be plagued with strings going out of tune. Change them at least 24 hours before a performance. If you are performing every day and like the sound of fresh, bright strings, then change them AFTER each performance to allow them to sit until the next day's gig.

Q: Is it okay to clip the strings in the middle to remove them?
A: Absolutely not! Especially if the string are up to pitch. The shock of a sudden release of tension could cause severe damage to the structure of the soundboard and/or bridge. You can only clip them in the middle when all of the tension has been relieved.

Q: Can I use tension as a reference to what kind of strings I need for my guitar?
A: Yes. If your instrument is usually weak-sounding on a certain string or group of strings, you can usually compensate for the deficiency by selecting a set that has higher tensions for those strings. Strings with higher tensions have a more dominant quality than those with lower tension. Strings with lower tension may tend to cause fret buzzes on instruments with low actions because the strings are looser and vibrate in larger cylindrical patterns.

Q: Are there any strings made that have the same tensions on each string in the set?
A: Gibson's Equa strings are carefully engineered to provide equal tensions on each string. These sets provide the most even response on instruments that use electromagnetic pickups to amplify the string's vibrations.

Q: What is the difference between heavy, hard, light and soft?
A: "Heavy" and "hard" don't always go hand in hand. Neither do "light" and "soft". Heavy-gauge strings aren't necessarily hard-playing strings, and not all light-gauge strings have a soft, easy feel. It's more important to look at the weight and stiffness of a strong — especially when evaluating wound strings. As mentioned earlier, you can use a variety of core/wrap combinations to make a string of a particular gauge. A .040" string made from a .016" core wire with a .012" wrap (.016" $ .012" $ .012" 5 .040") will have a softer playing feel than a .040" string made with a .020" core and a .010" wrap (.020" $ .010" $ .010" 5 .040"). The mass of each string will be similar, but the core wire of the second one is 20 % smaller is diameter and thus has a lighter fretting "feel".

Q: Why will phosphor-bronze strings work with a piezo transducer and not with a regular pickup?
A: The piezo transducer senses changes in its shape, to then effect the change in voltage necessary to reproduce the guitar's sound. Electromagnetic pickups sense the movement of a metallic object within their "field". Phosphor-bronze (also brass and copper, for that matter) cannot be sensed by the electromagnetic pickup. Instead, the pickup "reads" only the core wire and the amplified effect is very minimal.

Q: Can I save old strings and use them again?
A: Once the strings have been on an instrument for some time, they are stretched out and have lost their elasticity. The physical nature of the string has been changed and it cannot be revitalized.

Q: Is there a difference in sound between a string with high tension and one with low tension?
A: Yes. Strings with higher tension will tend to sound "stronger" and more "forceful" than strings with lower tension. Strings with lower tension will tend to sound "warmer", "fuller", and "rounder" than those with heavier tension.

Q: How can I reduce finger noise?
A: If you are playing electric guitar, you may wish to try some of the flat-wound strings. The polished surface offers less resistance and eliminates most of the finger "squeaks". If you play acoustic, a very light application of oil from your cleaning rag will help reduce noise. Once new strings are played a bit, their surfaces become slightly polished, and that will help to reduce noises too.

Q: Other than sound, are there other things I should consider when selecting a particular wrap wire?
A: Some strings with softer metals, such as copper in the alloys of their wrap wire are prone to wrap-wire wear. Sets with Monel wrap wire have a long life by comparison. The harder steel alloys may cause some fret wear on the instrument. In the final analysis, it is the quality of tone that you prefer, that is really most important.

Q: Is there one type of string that will work well on every kind of instrument?
A: Every instrument is different, for each and every piece of wood is different. Not every set of string will work well on every guitar. You have to select a set of strings that is exactly right for your particular needs.

Q: Should I slacken the strings when I put away my guitar?
A: No. Although you might lengthen the string's life a little, you will also shorten the guitar's life a great deal. The instrument is designed to withstand string tension. If it has a truss rod, then adjustments have probably been made by the manufacturer to counter the force of the strings. If you loosen the strings for a long period, you might cause neck adjustments to go out of alignment.

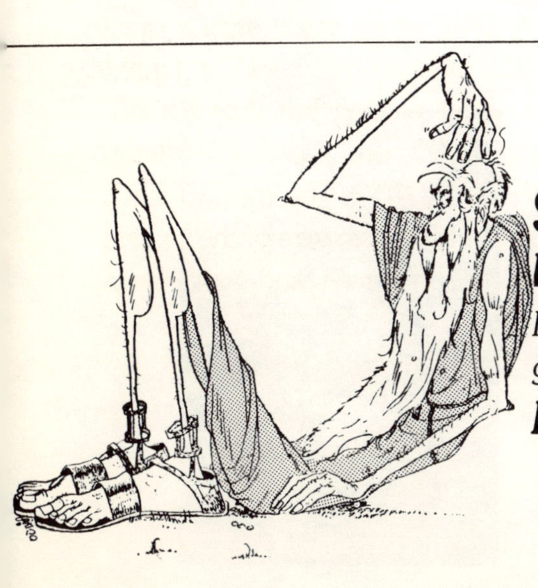

STRANGE FACT: #4
HE USED A LOADED GUITAR
In an old western movie Roy Rogers gunned down a bad guy with a guitar that had a gun hidden in the neck.
HE COULD HAVE USED LOADED STRINGS.

Other guitar books from CENTERSTREAM

GOSPEL GUITAR VOL. 2 00000031
"Flatpicking and Travis Style"
Arranged by Fred Sokolow, this book contains the SAME songs as the
GOSPEL BANJO VOL.2. Each song is written in Tab. and Music notation
in 3 ways and 3 keys--2 flatpicking and 1 Travis stlye. Partial contents: Can
The Circle Be Unbroken / Do Lord / Great Speckled Bird / It's Me, O Lord /
Leaning On The Everlasting Arsm / What A Friend We Have In Jesus /
When The Saints Go Marching In. and many more.

____ **POWER CHORDING - ROCK RHYTHM PATTERNS FOR GUITAR
BEGINNER TO ADVANCED 00000044**
Arranged by Ron Middlebrook. This book contains a wide range of Rock Rhythm
patterns for Guitarists, including: How To Play Bar Chords / Rhythm Lessons /
Locating Rhythm Patterns On Sheet Music / Light Rock Ballad Chording / Muting /
Hard Rock Chording / Latin Disco / Chuck Berry Style Chording / Bo Diddley Style
Chording / and more.

____ **SCALE POWER FOR GUITAR 00000044**
Modes, chord scales, improvisation, and patterns. This book takes you step by
step through the 7 modes: Ionian, Dorian, Phrygian, Lydian, Mixolydian, Aeolian
and Locrian. And the chords used to improvise with.

____ **SCALES AND MODES - IN THE BEGINNING (UPDATED)
00000010**
By Ron Middlebrook. The most comprehensive and complete scale book written
especially for the guitar. Newly updated with even more scale detail. Divided into 4
main sections: 1 - Fretboard Visualization, the breaking down of the whole into
parts. 2 - Scale Terminology, a thorough understanding of whole and half steps,
scale degrees, intervals, etc. 3 - Scales And Modes, the heart of the book, covers
every scale you'll ever need with exercises and applications. 4 - Scale To Chord
Guide, ties it all together, showing us what scale to use over various chords.

____ **FINGERPICKING DELIGHTS 00000051**
From the guitar repertoire of Stefan Grossman, Kicking Mule co-founder and
recording artist. Written in tablature and standard notation. Fiddle tunes, Ragtime,
Original and Blues songs. Includes a 20 minute record of Stefan playing plus tips
on how to play the songs correctly and "Guitar Player" magazine interview.

____ **FINGERSTYLE GUITAR SOLOS 00000019**
By fingerpicking expert Janet Smith. A method for the guitarist who is familiar with
the basic 1st position chords and would like to learn the art of the alternating bass.
The book includes instrumental solos in the fingerpicking style written in tablature
and in music notation. The 15 songs in several keys are Janet's own compositions
written essentially to illustrate commonly used riffs for solo playing. Most songs
are presented in two versions: a basic first-level version and one with fill-in notes
and syncopation for fuller sound. This book is an excellent starting point for
making up solos of your own. Sample contents: Poppy Seeds / Aspen By The Bay
/ Piano Mover's Rag / Nine Lives, Ten Fingers / Inside The Volcano.

____ **IRISH, SCOTTISH, ENGLISH AND AMERICAN FIDDLE TUNES
FOR THE FINGERPICKING GUITARIST 00000025**
By Duck Baker. Contains 125 pages of a wide variety of songs written in tablature
and standard notation with tips on picking, styles and special effects. Includes a
20 Min. record of Duck Baker playing the Reels. Breakdowns. Jigs. Slip Jigs.
Marches. Slow Airs. Hornpipes and much more. A must for every guitar player's
collection.

____ **GUITAR TUNING FOR THE COMPLETE MUSICAL IDIOT
(For Smart People Too!) 00000002**
By Ron Middlebrook. A complete book on how to tune up. With a tuning record
included. Contents include: Everything You Need To Know About Tuning, with
several methods explained / Intonation, what it is and how to set your guitar up /
Strings: how to find the right ones for you / 12 String Tuning / Picks, getting yours /
and much more.

____ **LEFT HAND GUITAR CHORD CHART 00000005**
Printed on durable card stock this "first-of-a-kind" guitar chord chart displays all
forms of major and minor chords in two forms.....beginner and advanced.

____ **OPEN GUITAR TUNINGS 00000037**
The only chart that illustrates 17 different tunings in easy to read diagrams.
Tunings for rock, blues, bluegrass, folk and country styles including open D (for
slide guitar), dropped D, Em, open C, modal tunings and many more.

____ **PICK & GRIN PATTERNS FOR GUITAR 00000039**
60 Different right hand patterns for pop, bluegrass, country, and folk guitar in easy
to read tablature. Includes left hand techniques for runs, endings etc.

____ **GRADED POSITION STUDIES FOR JAZZ GUITAR
00000022**
By Al Politano. "Get out of first position playing." No matter what your
playing level is — beginner to advanced — this super book is a major
step in playing in all the positions. The studies make use of every
common rhythm pattern, are melodious rather than exercise orientated,
and are completely fingered. In addition, the chords are included in
each graded study. (We recommend Al's book "Chords, Scales and
Arpeggios" for reference to the chords). If you're locked into the first 4
frets, and want to explore the whole fretboard, this is the book for you!

____ **RAY FLACKE SOLOS 00000085**
Exact off the record solos from Nashville's finest picker Ray
Flacke. Reveals for the first time the amazing guitar style that has
made his name synonymous with hot picking. Combination flat
and finger picking leads. Includes such hits as: HIGHWAY 40
BLUES / HEARTBREAK / ONE WAY RIDER / UNCLE PEN /
UNDER YOUR SPELL and more.

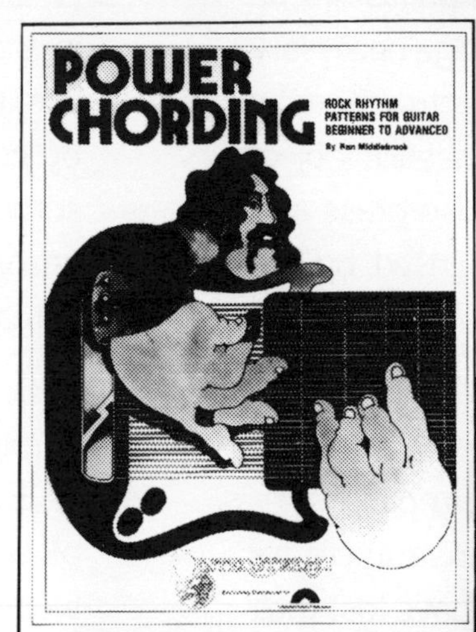

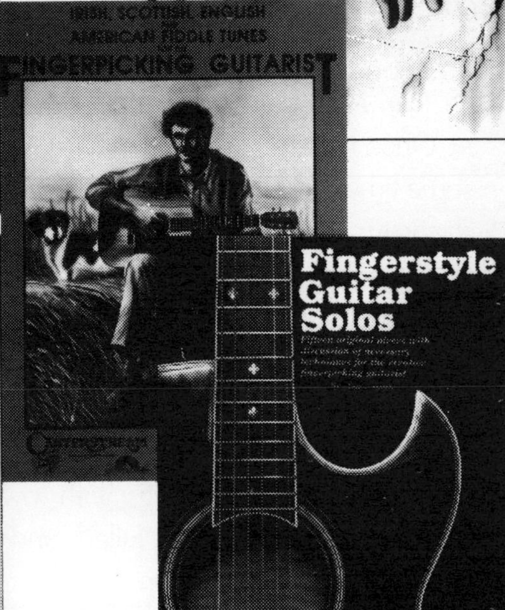

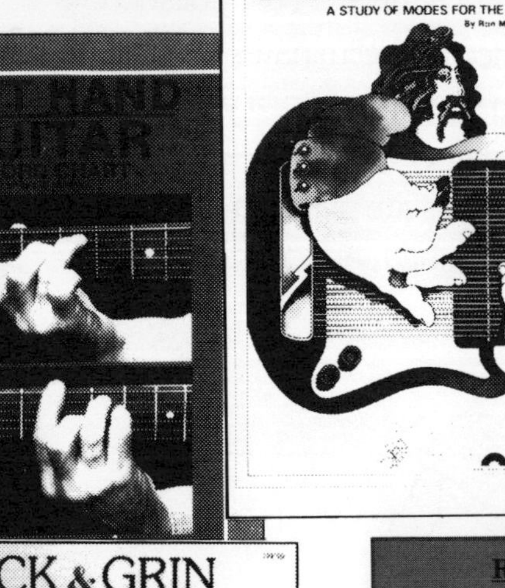